What About Health?

Food

by Fiona Waters

HODDER
Wayland

an imprint of Hodder Children's Books

Titles in the WHAT ABOUT HEALTH? series

Drugs

Exercise

Food

Hygiene

Food is a simplified version of the title
Food and Your Health in Wayland's 'Health Matters' series.

Language level consultant: Norah Granger
Editor: Belinda Hollyer
Designer: Jane Hawkins

First published in 2001 by Hodder Wayland,
an imprint of Hodder Children's Books.

Reprinted in 2002

British Library Cataloguing in Publication Data
Waters, Fiona
Food. - (What about health?)
1.Nutrition - Requirements - juvenile literature
I.Title
613.2
ISBN 0 7502 3612 4

Printed in Hong Kong

Hodder Children's Books
A division of Hodder Headline Limited
338 Euston Road, London NW1 3BH

Picture acknowledgements
Illustrations: Jan Sterling
Cover: all Hodder Wayland Picture Library; Cephas 5, 13 both, 18;
Chapel Studios 19, 25 top, 26; Greg Evans 15, 23, 25 bottom;
Impact 29 (Roger Scruton); J. Allan Cash 7, 17, 24; Tony Stone 10
(Gray Mortimore), 12 (Steve Outram); Hodder Wayland Picture
Library 4, 6, 9, 11, 14, 16, 20, 21, 22, 27, 28.

Contents

Food and your body   4

Eating your food   6

Food to help you grow   8

Food to keep you fit   10

Fats in food   12

Food and your weight   14

What is fibre?   16

What are vitamins and minerals?   18

Food and your teeth   20

Food with extra colour and taste   22

Food can make you ill   24

Keeping food fresh and clean   26

What you should eat to keep well   28

Glossary   30

Finding out more   31

Index   32

Food and your body

You need to eat food to stay alive.
Good food makes your body work
well. Food keeps you warm.
Food makes you strong.

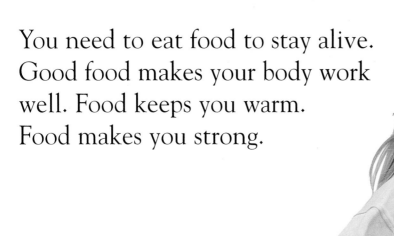

Oranges are
good for your
bones and skin.

Meat and fish
make you strong.

Cheese keeps you
warm and gives
you energy.

Bread and
potatoes help
you run fast.

THESE FOODS ARE GOOD FOR YOU

Butter, milk and cheese

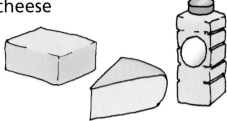

Meat, fish and beans

Bread, potatoes and pasta

Fruit and vegetables

▼ Good food keeps you healthy.

Cut out pictures of your favourite food from magazines. Stick them on a card. Do you think your favourite foods are good for you?

Eating your food

When you eat, you bite into your food. Your teeth break the food into little bits. The juices in your mouth make the food soft. Then you swallow, and the food goes into your stomach. There it is mashed up with more juices. It then moves into your small intestine. Your body keeps all the good bits. The rest goes into the large intestine. You get rid of this waste when you go to the toilet.

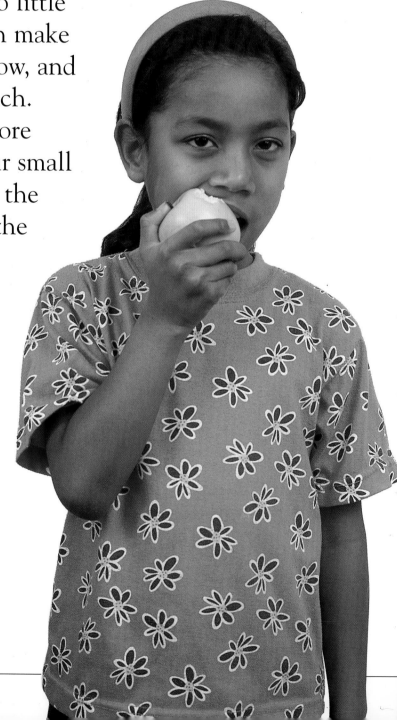

Your teeth break food into little bits. ▶

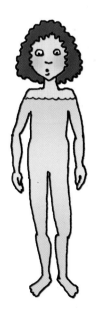

◀ Most of your body is water.

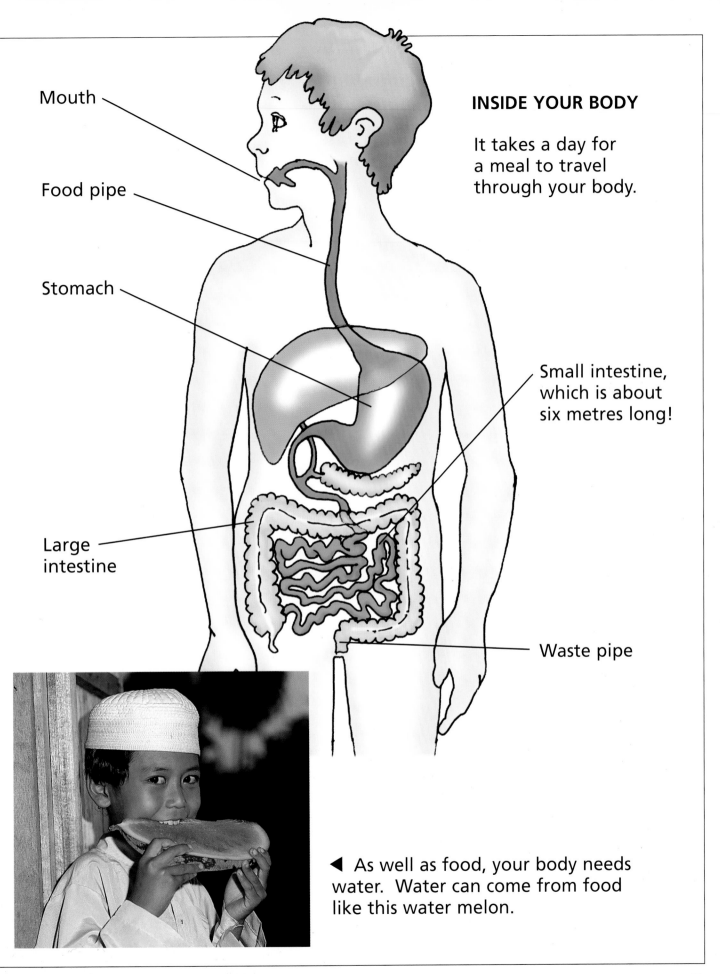

Mouth

Food pipe

Stomach

Large intestine

INSIDE YOUR BODY

It takes a day for a meal to travel through your body.

Small intestine, which is about six metres long!

Waste pipe

◀ As well as food, your body needs water. Water can come from food like this water melon.

Food to help you grow

Your body is made of millions of tiny parts. These parts are called cells. You need to make new cells all the time. Food helps make these cells. Meat and fish make new cells. So do eggs, cheese and milk. They all help make muscles and hair and skin.

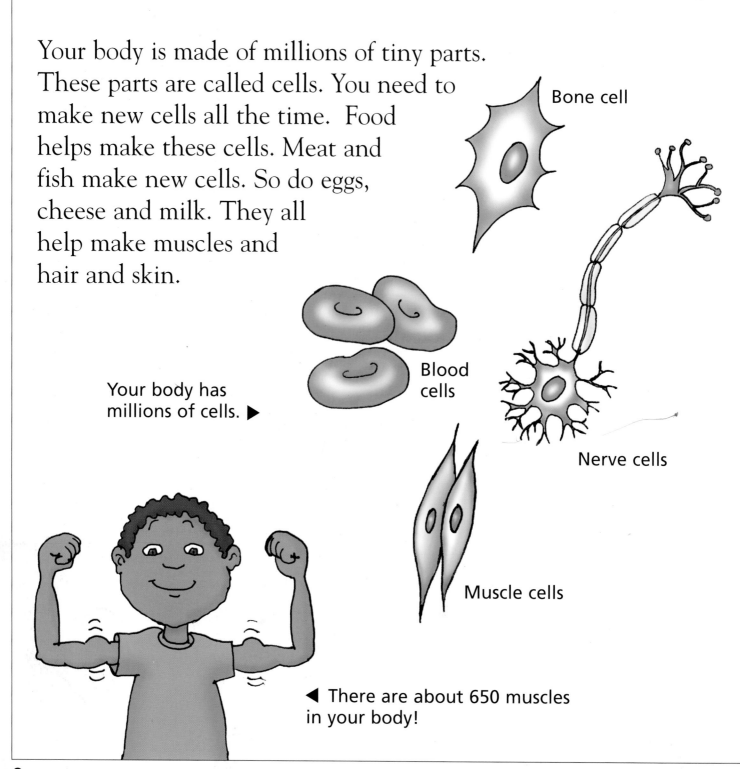

Bone cell

Blood cells

Nerve cells

Your body has millions of cells. ▶

Muscle cells

◀ There are about 650 muscles in your body!

YOUR BLOOD SYSTEM

The red lines show the tubes that carry blood away from your heart. The blue lines show the tubes that carry blood back to your heart.

Heart

Liver

Kidneys

Lungs

Stomach

Blood carries all the good parts of food around your body. They are stored in your liver.

You keep growing until you are about 18 ▼ years old.

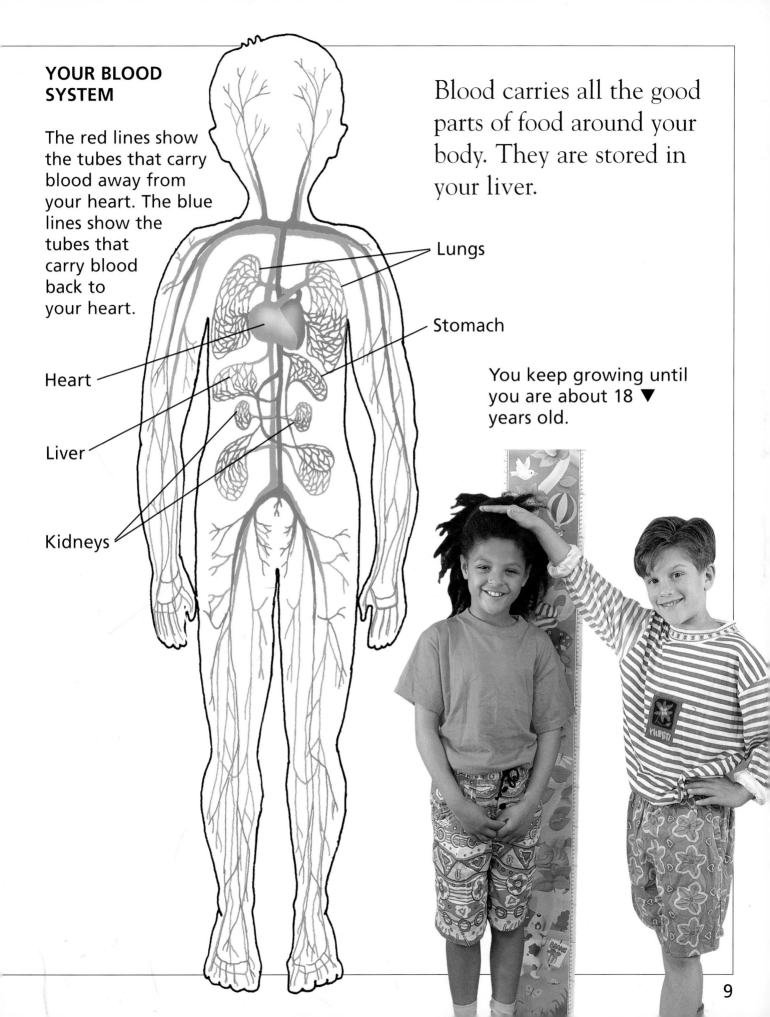

Food to keep you fit

Some foods help you to grow. Some foods keep you fit.

Potatoes, pasta, bread and rice help you run fast. They give you lots of energy. You should eat one of these with every meal.

▼ You need to be fit to run fast.

We rate the energy in foods by a measure called a calorie. If you eat 100 calories you can dance for ten minutes!

These foods contain 100 calories. ▼

50g bread	100g bananas	20g nuts	1½ apples

Potatoes are very good for you. They taste good too!
▼

You need to eat lots of calories every day.

Boys need 2400 – 2800

Girls need 2200 – 2400

Boys usually need more because they are often bigger than girls.

Fats in food

Your body needs some fat to keep warm. Some people eat too much fat. If you are too fat, your heart can't work properly.

You can see the fat on meat or chips. Cakes and biscuits and ice-cream contain fat you can't see.

Tuna fish is full of oily fat. This helps the blood move round your body. The fat on meat or cream makes your blood sticky so it moves too slowly.

FATS THAT HELP YOUR HEART
Olive oil
Fish oil
Sunflower oil

FATS THAT CAN HARM YOUR HEART
Milk
Cream
Butter
Bacon

Oily fish are good for you. The fat in them helps your heart. ▶

EAT LESS FAT

Jacket potatoes not chips

Jacket potatoes	less fat
Chips	more fat

Yoghurt not cream

Yoghurt	less fat
Cream	more fat

Chicken not beef

Chicken	less fat
Beef	more fat

▲ Stirfried food has less fat than fried food.

Oil can come from the seeds of sunflowers.▼

Make a list of what you eat each day. Do you think you might eat too much fat?

Food and your weight

You need to eat enough food to be the right weight. If you eat too much you will put on too much weight. If you eat too little you will get ill. It is not good to be too fat or too thin.

Pasta and potatoes, and vegetables and fruit, do not make you fat. Too much sugar and fat will make you put on weight.

▲ Find out if you are the right weight. Your weight will change as you grow.

◄ If you eat too much fat it will be stored under your skin.

GOOD FOOD IDEAS

● Eat three meals a day
● Don't miss a meal
● Eat lots of bread and pasta
● Eat lots of fruit and vegetables

Too much fat and sugar will make you weigh too much. ▶

THIS PICTURE SHOWS YOU HOW MUCH TO EAT OF DIFFERENT FOODS

● Bread, pasta and potatoes
● Meat and fish
● Fat and sugar

● Milk and cheese
● Fruit and vegetables

What is fibre?

Fibre is what is left when all the good bits of what you eat have been taken away. It can help your blood flow around your body. Fibre pushes all the waste through your body when you go to the toilet.

Fibre comes from fruit and vegetables. It also comes from rice and breakfast cereals.

Wild rice and brown rice have more fibre than white rice.▼

THESE FOODS HAVE NO FIBRE
eggs
fruit drinks
fish
ice-cream

FOOD WITH LOTS OF FIBRE

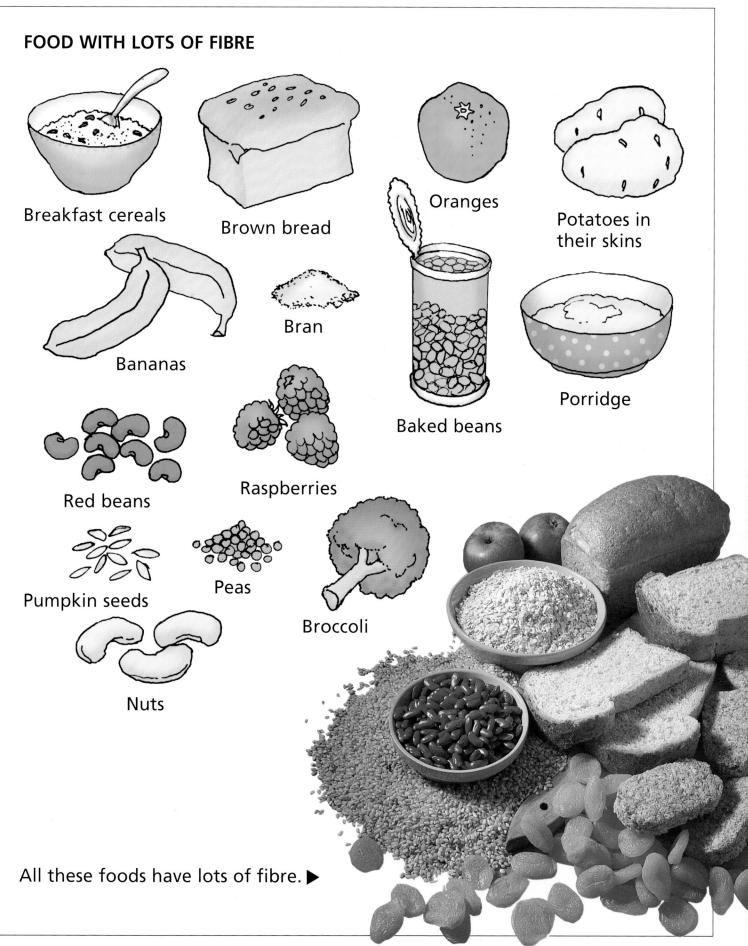

Breakfast cereals

Brown bread

Oranges

Potatoes in their skins

Bananas

Bran

Baked beans

Porridge

Red beans

Raspberries

Pumpkin seeds

Peas

Broccoli

Nuts

All these foods have lots of fibre. ▶

What are vitamins and minerals?

You can't see vitamins and minerals. They are in the food you eat. If you do not have enough, your body will not work well.

The vitamins have letters as names. Vitamin C helps you fight colds. Vitamin K helps cuts to get better. Salt is a mineral. So is calcium, which makes your teeth and bones strong. Iron is a mineral that makes your blood healthy.

▼ Raw fruit and vegetables have lots of minerals.

VITAMINS AND MINERALS ARE FOUND IN THESE FOODS

Vitamin A
butter, eggs, carrots

Vitamin B1
milk, bread, meat, vegetables

Vitamin B2
milk, cheese, eggs, meat, vegetables

Vitamin C
oranges, tomatoes, peppers

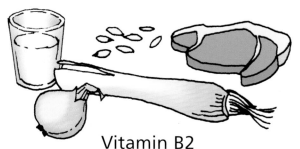

Vitamin D
oily fish, eggs, nuts, vegetables

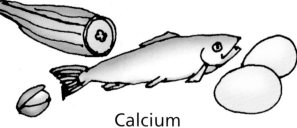

Calcium
milk, cheese, bread

Iron
sardines, beef, liver

▲ A glass of milk has lots of vitamins and calcium.

Salt is a mineral. We need some salt every day, but many people eat too much salt.

Food and your teeth

It is bad for your teeth if you eat too much sugar. Tiny living things eat the bits of food left in your mouth. These tiny things are called bacteria. If the bacteria get inside a tooth they will make it rot away.

Apples and carrots help keep your teeth clean.
▼

Most people eat their own weight in sugar every year.

You should always clean your teeth after eating sweets. ▶

TOOTH RULES

- Brush your teeth twice a day
- Get a new tooth brush every two months
- Use floss between your teeth
- See the dentist twice a year

Lots of foods have hidden sugar. The labels on the tins and packets will tell you how much sugar each food has.

Food with extra colour and taste

A lot of the food we buy is ready to eat. Some of it has an extra colour or taste put in. These extras are called additives. They make the food last longer and look nicer. Additives make the colours brighter. They make the taste stronger.

Some colours come from plants. Some tastes are made in factories.

NATURAL PLANT COLOURS

Orange comes from carrots. Red comes from beetroot.

You can read the labels to find out what has been added to food. ▶

THESE FOODS HAVE ALL HAD EXTRA COLOUR OR TASTE ADDED

Ham, bacon, sausages
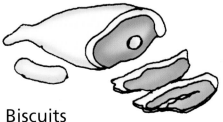

Pie fillings

Soup from packets

Biscuits

Sandwich fillings

Soft drinks

▲ These sweets have had colours added to them.

You can look at the labels on tins to see if they contain different additives.

23

Food can make you ill

There are people who cannot eat some foods because they make them ill. Foods like milk, eggs and peanuts can make some people sick. Other people get very ill if they eat too much sugar. The wheat in bread, cakes and biscuits can make some people sick, too. Added colours and tastes can also cause problems.

▼ This bread could make some people very ill.

SOME PEOPLE CANNOT EAT THESE FOODS

prawns

mussels
nuts

strawberries
milk
eggs

bananas

▲ Some people don't eat meat because of their beliefs.

RELIGION AND FOOD

Hindus and Buddhists will not eat beef.

Muslims and Jews will not eat pork.

Some religions also have rules about how food is prepared and cooked.

Some food can bring you out in a rash.

Some people never eat meat or fish. They are called vegetarians.

Keeping food fresh and clean

If you eat food that is not fresh it can make you sick. Some foods, such as meat, cheese and milk, must be kept in a fridge. Cooked and uncooked food should be kept apart.

Fruit and salads must be washed before you eat them. Meat must be cooked right to the middle to kill any bacteria. Bacteria can make you very ill.

Thousands of bacteria could fit on to the top of a pin.▼

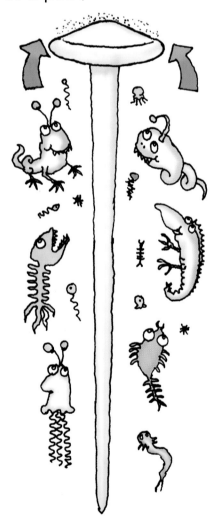

◀ You should wash vegetables very well.

◀ All this food has gone bad. You can see the mould on it.

FRESH FOOD RULES

- You must wash your hands before you eat
- Keep the kitchen clean
- Don't cough over food
- Keep pets and flies away from your food

Read the labels on some jars and packets. Make a list of where you should keep food like milk, biscuits, baked beans, and ice-cream. How long can you store them?

What you should eat to keep well

You need to eat lots of different foods to keep well. Too many sweets and crisps are not good for you. More and more people today are eating organic food. Organic food is food farmed with almost no chemicals added to the soil.

Ice-cream is a lovely treat, but too much is not good for you. ▶

WHAT TO EAT TO BE FIT

There are five main kinds of food.

1. Potatoes, pasta, rice

2. Milk, butter, cheese

3. Fruit and vegetables

4. Meat and fish

5. Cakes and biscuits

The first four kinds of food are best for you. The fifth kind should only be a treat now and again.

These potatoes are growing on an organic farm. ▶

We call burgers and fries fast food. The best fast food is an apple. Draw a picture of yourself eating an apple. Do you know why an apple is good for you?

Glossary

Bacteria   Tiny living things. Some can make you very sick, but others are good for you.

Calcium   A mineral which makes strong teeth and bones.

Calories   We measure the energy in food by counting the calories in it.

Cells   The millions of little parts that make up your body.

Fat   The part of food which keeps you warm.

Fibre   What is left of your food when all the good bits have been taken away.

Intestine   The long tube that takes food from your stomach.

Minerals   The goodness found in food which you need to keep healthy. One important mineral in food is iron.

Muscles   Muscles move your bones when you exercise.

Organic food   Food farmed with hardly any chemicals being added.

Vegetarian   A person who does not eat meat or fish.

Vitamins   The goodness found in food which you need to keep healthy. One important vitamin is Vitamin C.

Finding out more

BOOKS TO READ

Diet and Health by Ida Weeks (Wayland, 1991)

Healthy Food by Anne Qualter and John Quinn (Wayland, 1993)

Poultry by Jillian Powell (Wayland, 1997)

Vegetables by Jillian Powell (Wayland, 1997)

ORGANIZATIONS

Health Development Agency

(this used to be called the Health Education Authority)

Trevelyan House, 30 Great Peter Street

London SW1P 2HW

Telephone 020 7222 5300

Website www.hea.org.uk

Index

additives 22, 23, 24

bacteria 20, 26
blood 8, 9, 12, 16, 18
bone cells 8
Buddhists 25

calcium 7, 18, 19
calories 11
cells 8, 18
colourings 22, 23, 24

eating 6, 10, 11
energy 4, 10, 11,

fats 4, 12, 13, 14, 15, 22
fibre 16, 17
flavourings 22, 24

germs 26

heart 9, 12
Hindus 25

intestines 6, 7

Jews 25

liver 7, 9

minerals 18, 19
muscles 8
Muslims 25

nerve cells 8

oil 12, 13
organic food 28, 29

religion 25

stomach 6, 7
sugar 14, 15, 20, 21, 24,

teeth 6, 18, 20, 21
toilet 6, 16

vegetarians 25
vitamins 18, 19

waste 6, 16
water 6, 7
weight 14, 15